20 Shots From The Quiver

20 Shots From The Quiver

JOHN HENRY DAM

InfusedMedia Co. LLC
www.infusedmedia.co
1-888-251-6088

For You On Mother's Day

Thank You Mother for being loving and respectable, predominately merciful, tender, and soothing.

Thank You Mother for possessing valor and persevering the most arduous tasks encountered.

Thank You Mother for functioning as a supervisor, and deciphering problems at hand, while rectifying the wrong.

Thank You Mother for striving to be adept at whatever Your endeavor may be and being the best!

Thank You Mother at day's end for the kiss on the brow, assuring the night would be a good night and that "You" would see all in the morning.

Mother, Loving You Is Easy To Do!

"HAPPY MOTHERS DAY"

I Pray

We will be-what-in-you I see

My desire for You and Your desire for me

I want present as well as receive

A shoulder to lean on

Mine for You and Yours for Me

The Joy we share will prompt a smile

Small problems of yours- are- bigger to me

I am trusting in You- In me you trust too

In Our life the Lord is found

No doubt we will be Heaven bound

Days without strife

This My agenda for life

I await to hold

What I know I have found

Look carefully you may see

And too, witness this in Me!

Your Beauty I Hear

Oh my ears-Your beauty-The sound they See.

A smile-Those eyes-They grin at me.

Mealtime!-Important?-Not to me!

A call-Your Voice-a Beautiful sight to see!

Like Neon lights-sweet-I hear a symphony.

A Bequest, my request-I pray-He answers me!

Ty's Dad!

Found out who and what I am

Crashing his car departing from time

Given a name of egoism

Me

People look saying

That's Ty's Dad

It makes me sad

Tagged with it, I'm proud I'm glad

And Relaying my greatest feelings of self-esteem

I'm Ty's dad!

Thoughts

Of you, thoughts in mind

About you, it's hard without you

With you, thoughts were kind

From you a "Hey"! Your way of saying Hi!

To "Later"! You'd say

Your way of good-bye

Along with an "I love you" and a hug

The center of the pie!

Sweet Memories

Memories yours are many

They will always be alive

Such as honey bees are many

That live in a hive

Like God's creatures they work

And work all the time

Results being the sweet taste of time!

My Son His Dad

Father and Son

Awesome were TWO, Connecting Mind and Soul

A Right that was Wrong

Then a Wrong that was Right

Single in Conception, Thoughts of TWO

Approval Coveted, Inspirational

Saturnine, Rejection

Suicide a Temptation

An Aberration, Dismissed!

TWO that was ONE

Is now ONE recalling TWO

WISHING, WANTING, LOVING MY SON

HIS DAD !

My Pretty Perfect Princess

As Butterflies while fleeing

Your beautiful in being

Soaring above the usual

Is your flight of Elation

For all to receive

Beauty is the sight

And relative is their delight!

He She And Me

Death Before Life -He is My Son

Above and Beyond He has journeyed

With Drawn-but not from

I Feel Him In Every Way

She came to me His schoolmate

An Angel He Sent to Me

His Friend is Now My Ally

I love Her-No Better One Can Be

Touching Him is not possible

We Converse Everyday

I Question-Again If I'll Hug Him

I Miss Him In Every Way

She No Doubt Is From Heaven

She Picks Me up When I'm Down

He Was a Prince an Angel

This Connection is of three

He She and Me!

Forever My Love

Thoughts of you "Linger"
They are features of the Mind
Reminiscent is perfume
On a balmy Summer Night
Half leaves and withers
Fading in the dark
Timeless is the other,
Never will it part.

Euphoria at Least

Anticipation, escalation, powering the heart it seems.

Clarification, transformation, infatuation new found to me.

A cheek a kiss then major bliss changing me heatedly.

Scared of losing you, never having you, what's wrong with me?

Tummies hollow, hard to swallow, hope you're thinking of me!

What an evening, love, a feeling quite appealing, hope it stays.

Love a power from above, hovering, such as grace of a dove.

Good may come, the worst will go, later the best will show.

I will be yours, will you be mine, to the last twinkle of time!

Not here to beg or steal, but to offer a life to death deal?

QUEEN-will you rumble with my bumble so we can BEE?!

I Understand

Bringing you to me

He cast a light to see

Receiving is more than wanting

Meeting you this I found

Looking at you I saw

Inside of me it took to see

Permanent is endless

Indefinite is a short

Timeless with an end!

An Ode To Tyler

Memories Like Crickets; Similar
Heard Not Seen; Hidden
Hugs, and Hand Shakes; Thoughts
Energized At Night; Silence
Departing In Times Light; Barely!

Hallowed Thoughts

Inherent elegance a vision of thee

Dignity and decency an aura to see

Commanding respect an air to be

Warm the persona then following

A Goddess-You- and were sent to

ME!

A Real Cowboys Misfortune

Beneficial the look but crucial it isn't

You are born a cowboy Iike it or not

A gift from at birth blessed by God

Each is distinct but a comparable lot

They treat women as Ladies

An honor given-Deserving or not

They don't waver when committing to favor

One's problem Belongs to all

All problems belong to one.

From beginning to end they are one

To finish from start

You find one as one-hundred

Or one hundred as one

Each one is different but alike the whole

Ask them for help and they will bestowal.

Aspiring Valentine

Oh, my ears, the beauty, the sight they see.

A smile-Those Eyes-They grin at me.

Mealtime! -Important? -Not to me!

A call-Your Voice-a Beautiful sight to see!

Like Neon lights-sweet-I hear a symphony.

A Bequest, my request-I Pray-He answers me!

Will You Be My Valentine?

Spontaneous

Reaction, to an action, an effect of a cause.
The after that's here after
and there after its gone!

Justification

Laying then lying, taking a chance, not knowing is not hurting

a fairy tail romance!

No End In Sight

Two decades of torture, termination, a hallucination!

Daily tormented, encompassing love not in scope.

Interim, juvenility to day present, unwilling and burdensome.

A voracious craving to apprehend, for naught.

Expectation, anticipation elevate aspirations to survive.

Half-baked me! Half-hearted you, omissions is not an option!

Questionable

Will it be remembered the way it really was, or is the way it really was the way it really is?

A Step to Succeed

Success is possible only if there is hope and to have hope you must have a dream so consequently without a dream failure is inevitable.